This coloring book belongs to:

_____

If ye will have
faith in me ye
shall have power
to do whatsoever
thing is
expedient in me

Moroni 7:33

❁

I will
go and do
the things which
the Lord
hath
commanded.

❁

1 Nephi 3:7

✻

Faith is
things which
are hoped
for and not
seen.

✻

Ether 12:6

✻

As many as should look upon the Son of God with faith might live.

✻

Helaman 8:15

❋

The Lord is
able to do all
things for the
children of men,
if they exercise
faith in him.

❋

1 Nephi 7:12

✳

The pointers in the Liahona
worked according to faith.

✳

1 Nephi 16:28

❀

If they have faith in me, then will I make weak things become strong unto them.

❀

Ether 12:27-28

✽

Repent, and be baptized in
his name, having perfect faith
in the Holy One,

✽

2 Nephi 9:23

❁

Christ works
mighty miracles
among the
children of men
according to their
faith.

❁

2 Nephi 26:13

All they who wrought miracles wrought them by faith.

Ether 12:12–18

❀

And he hath
said: Repent all ye ends of
the earth, and come unto me,
and be baptized in my name,
and have faith in me, that ye
may be saved.

❀

Moroni 7:34

✿

*Whatsoever thing ye
shall ask the Father
in my name, which is
good, in faith believing
that ye shall receive,
behold, it shall be
done unto you.*

✿

Moroni 7:26

✽

For no man can be saved,
according to the words of
Christ, save they shall have
faith in his name;

✽

Moroni 7:38

✳

And he said unto
me: Because of thy faith in
Christ, whom thou hast never
before heard nor seen. And
many years pass away before he
shall manifest himself in the
flesh; wherefore, go to, thy faith
hath made thee whole.

✳

Enos 1:3-8

❋

Salvation cometh to none such
except it be through faith on
the Lord Jesus Christ.

❋

Mosiah 3:12

✻

Hearts are changed through faith on his name.

✻

Mosiah 5:7

✽

Give us strength according to our faith in Christ.

✽

Alma 14:26

❋

Call on God's name in faith.

❋

Alma 22:16

✻

Faith is not to have a
perfect knowledge of things.

✻

Alma 32:21

❁

As it beginneth to swell even so nourish it by your faith,

❁

Alma 33:23

❁

Their preservation was ascribed to the miraculous power of God because of their exceeding faith.

❁

Alma 57:25-27

✻

I see that your faith is sufficient
that I should heal you.

✻

3 Nephi 17:8

✤

*If ye shall ask, having
faith in Christ, he will
manifest the truth.*

✤

Moroni 10:4

✻

As it beginneth to swell even so nourish it by your faith,

✻

Alma 33:28

✱

They who have faith in
Christ will cleave unto every
good thing.

✱

Moroni 7:28

❋

The prayers of God's servants
are answered according to
their faith.

❋

Mosiah 27:14

Made in the USA
Monee, IL
09 September 2021

77740414R00031